HOW TO DRAW COMIC BOOK HEROES

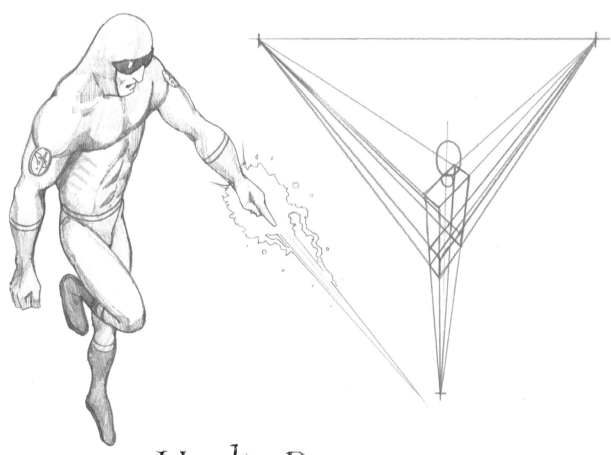

Mark Bergin

PowerKiDS
press.

New York

Published in 2011 by The Rosen Publishing Group, Inc.
29 East 21st Street, New York, NY 10010

Editor: Rob Walker
U.S. Editor: Kara Murray

Library of Congress Cataloging-in-Publication Data

Bergin, Mark.
  How to draw comic book heroes / Mark Bergin. — 1st ed.
     p. cm.
  Includes index.
   ISBN 978-1-4488-1579-1 (library binding)
 ISBN 978-1-4488-1604-0 (pbk.) —
 ISBN 978-1-4488-1605-7 (6-pack)
  1. Superheroes in art—Juvenile literature. 2. Comic strip—
 characters—Juvenile literature. 3. Figure drawing—Technique.
 I. Title.
   NC1764.8.H47B47 2011
   741.5'1—dc22
                        2010007157

Manufactured in Heshan, China

CPSIA Compliance Information: Batch #SS0102PK: For Further Information contact
Rosen Publishing, New York, New York at 1-800-237-9932

Contents

Making a Start

Learning to draw is about looking and seeing. Keep practicing and get to know your subject. Use a sketchbook to make quick drawings. Start by doodling and experimenting with shapes and patterns. There are many ways to draw, and this book shows only some methods. Visit art galleries, look at artists' drawings, and see how your friends draw, but above all, find your own way.

You can practice drawing figures using an artist's model—a wooden figure that can be put into various poses.

When drawing from photos, use construction lines to help you understand the form of the body and how each of its parts relate to each other.

Practice sketching people in everyday surroundings. This will help you draw faster and train you to capture the main elements of a pose quickly.

Try sketching friends and family at home.

You can create new poses by drawing simple stick figures.

5

Perspective

If you look at a figure from different viewpoints, you will see that whichever part is closest to you looks larger, and the part farthest away from you looks smallest. Drawing in perspective is a way of creating a feeling of depth—of suggesting three dimensions on a flat surface.

V.P.

The vanishing point (V.P.) is the place in a perspective drawing where parallel lines appear to meet. The position of the vanishing point depends on the viewer's eye level.

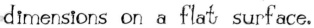

V.P.

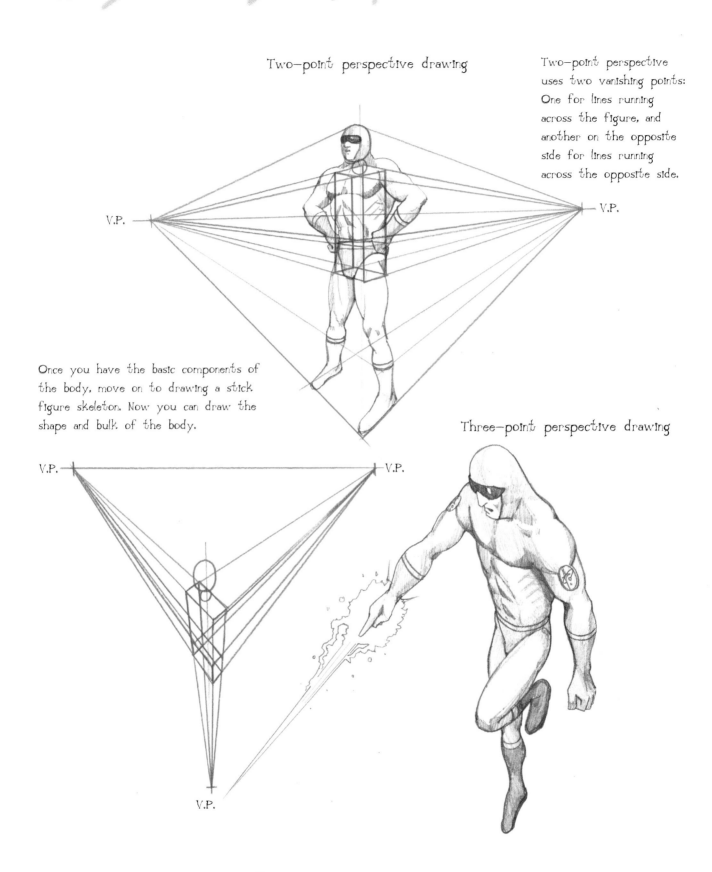

Two-point perspective drawing

Two-point perspective uses two vanishing points: One for lines running across the figure, and another on the opposite side for lines running across the opposite side.

V.P.

V.P.

Once you have the basic components of the body, move on to drawing a stick figure skeleton. Now you can draw the shape and bulk of the body.

V.P.

V.P.

Three-point perspective drawing

V.P.

Three-point perspective drawings use three vanishing points. This method is good for drawing objects at more dramatic angles.

V.P. = vanishing point

7

Drawing Materials

Try using different types of drawing papers and materials. Experiment with charcoal, wax crayons, and pastels. All pens, from felt-tips to ballpoints, will make interesting marks. Try drawing with pen and ink on wet paper for a variety of results.

Silhouette is a style of drawing that uses only a solid black shadow.

Ink

Felt-tip

Charcoal is very soft and can be used for big, bold drawings. Ask an adult to spray your charcoal drawings with fixative to prevent smudging.

You can create special effects in a drawing done with **wax crayons** by scraping parts of the color away.

8

Hard **pencil** leads are grayer and soft pencil leads are blacker. Pencils are graded from #1 (the softest) to #4 (the hardest).

Pencil

Ink

Pastels are even softer than charcoal and come in a wide range of colors. Ask an adult to spray your pastel drawings with fixative to prevent smudging.

Lines drawn in ink cannot be erased, so keep your ink drawings sketchy and less rigid. Don't worry about mistakes as these lines can be lost in the drawing as it develops.

Flying Superhero

The flying pose is a classic image of the superhero genre. The figure is often shown with an outstretched arm, clenched fist, and is usually wearing a cape to add dynamism to the pose.

The helmet worn by this hero has a finlike design.

The cape should be drawn billowing out behind the character.

Draw the hero's clenched fist.

Shade the inside of the cape.

Use different perspectives to change how the character moves.

Adding movement lines gives the character a sense of speed.

As the character in this drawing is flying away, more of the cape can be seen.

Add curved lines to show the folds in the cape. This gives the impression of it rippling through the air.

When drawing the hero flying straight toward you, you can include more detail in the facial expression, adding to the character.

Add movement lines.

11

Adapting Characters

These simple figures can be adapted to become any costumed hero striking a heroic pose. Here they can be seen as spies, sci-fi warriors, or superheroes.

Draw the basic shape of the figures using simple lines and ovals.

Spies

Using the basic figure, draw the hands, hair, and facial details. Then add the details of the spies' costumes and accessories.

Add hi-tech glasses and microphones.

Draw the belt with pouches.

Draw a bag slung around the shoulder and hanging at waist level.

Using curved lines draw a long coat on the female spy.

Sci-fi warriors

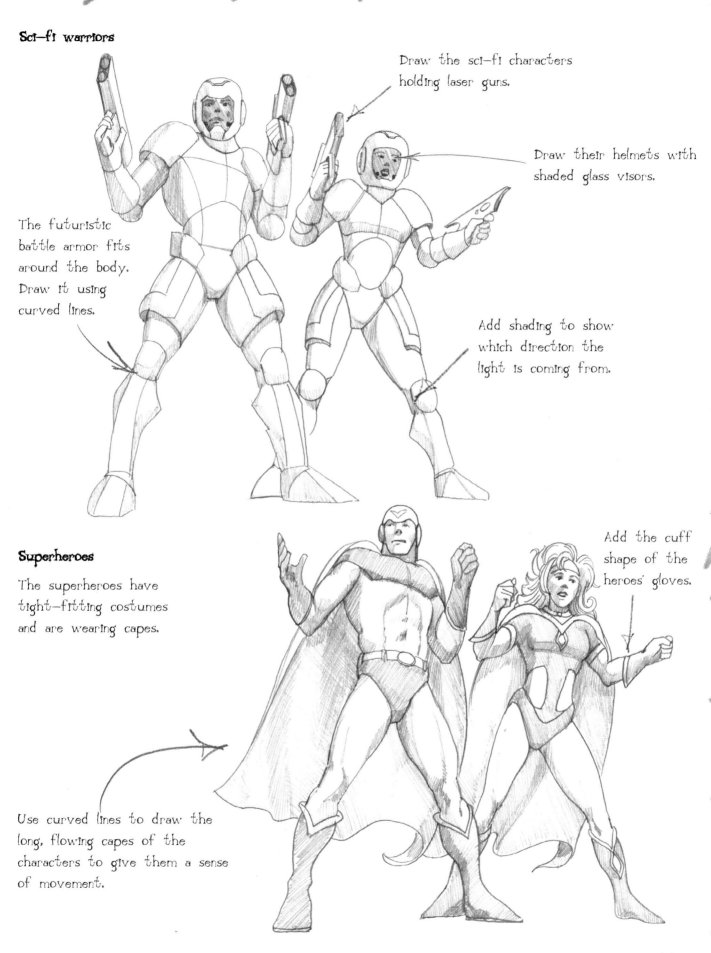

Draw the sci-fi characters holding laser guns.

Draw their helmets with shaded glass visors.

The futuristic battle armor fits around the body. Draw it using curved lines.

Add shading to show which direction the light is coming from.

Superheroes

The superheroes have tight-fitting costumes and are wearing capes.

Add the cuff shape of the heroes' gloves.

Use curved lines to draw the long, flowing capes of the characters to give them a sense of movement.

13

Good vs. Bad

Every superhero needs a super villain to battle against! The details of a character's face and costume can instantly place them on the side of good or evil.

Here are some pretty evil character designs.

This set of super villains look ready to do evil. Note their rough and menacing appearance with torn, ragged capes and unfriendly looks.

The superheroes' looks are the opposite to those of the villains. They look clean and virtuous.

In this action scene, the hero fights the villain. The villain's immense size helps create a sense of intimidation and the scale of evil that must be overcome.

The hero is using his superpowers to throw energy bolts at the villain.

Add details, such as hair and bindings, and any costumes.

Try to capture the sense of movement in your drawings with the use of dramatic poses.

This dynamic pose shows the hero dealing out justice to a super villain scientist.

The strange circuit design on the villain's costume and test tube in his hand suggest he is a mad scientist.

Use perspective to add to the drama of the scene.

Running Man

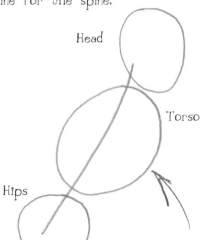

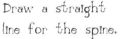
Draw a straight line for the spine.

The running man uses his power of super speed to rescue those in peril and catch the villains.

Head

Torso

Hips

Add three ovals: one each for the head, torso, and hips. The torso oval is much longer.

Draw small circles for the shoulders.

Sketch two cylinders to show the direction of the arms.

Draw a large ellipse for each thigh.

Add the lower section of each leg.

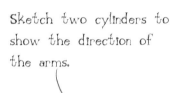

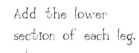
Draw the basic shape and direction of the feet.

Action Poses

Drawing basic stick figures can help you decide on a character's pose and what he might be doing.

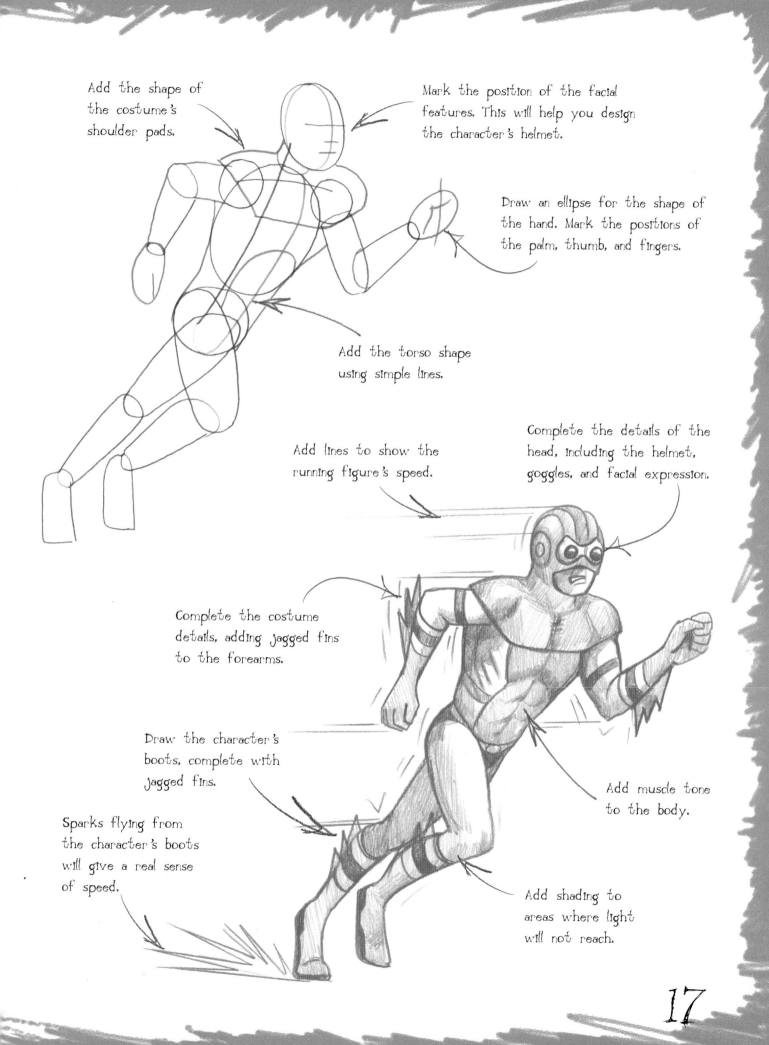

Add the shape of
the costume's
shoulder pads.

Mark the position of the facial
features. This will help you design
the character's helmet.

Draw an ellipse for the shape of
the hand. Mark the positions of
the palm, thumb, and fingers.

Add the torso shape
using simple lines.

Complete the details of the
head, including the helmet,
goggles, and facial expression.

Add lines to show the
running figure's speed.

Complete the costume
details, adding jagged fins
to the forearms.

Draw the character's
boots, complete with
jagged fins.

Add muscle tone
to the body.

Sparks flying from
the character's boots
will give a real sense
of speed.

Add shading to
areas where light
will not reach.

17

Super Strong Man

Super strength is a trait often found in superheroes. This character fights evil using his strength to overcome all odds. Here he can be seen lifting a huge boulder over his head.

Draw a straight line for the character's spine.

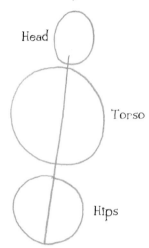

Head

Torso

Hips

Add three circles for the head, torso, and hips. Make the torso shape larger.

Add a small circle for each shoulder.

Add powerful thighs coming out from the hip circle.

Draw cylindrical shapes for the position of each arm.

Draw the shape of the lower legs, overlapping them with the thighs where the knee joints would be.

Sketch the basic shape and direction of the feet.

Draw a teardrop shape for each hand, remembering to think about how the hands would grasp the boulder.

Mark the position of the facial features.

Draw the basic shape of the figure's torso.

Draw a large rugged boulder.

Give your drawing added action by adding small fragments of rock falling off the boulder.

Complete the details of the hero's face and torso. Make sure he has a well-defined muscle structure under his costume.

Draw a large shadow under the hero, as the huge boulder casts a shadow, too.

19

Hi-Tech Spy

The hi-tech spy lives in the dangerous and exciting world of espionage. She needs all the latest equipment and technology to stay on top and survive.

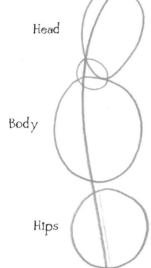

Head

Body

Hips

Draw four ellipses, one each for the head, neck, body, and hips.

Draw the shoulders with two small circles, joined with a straight line.

Sketch the position of the facial features.

Draw the legs of the spy.

Overlap both sections of each leg to indicate the joints.

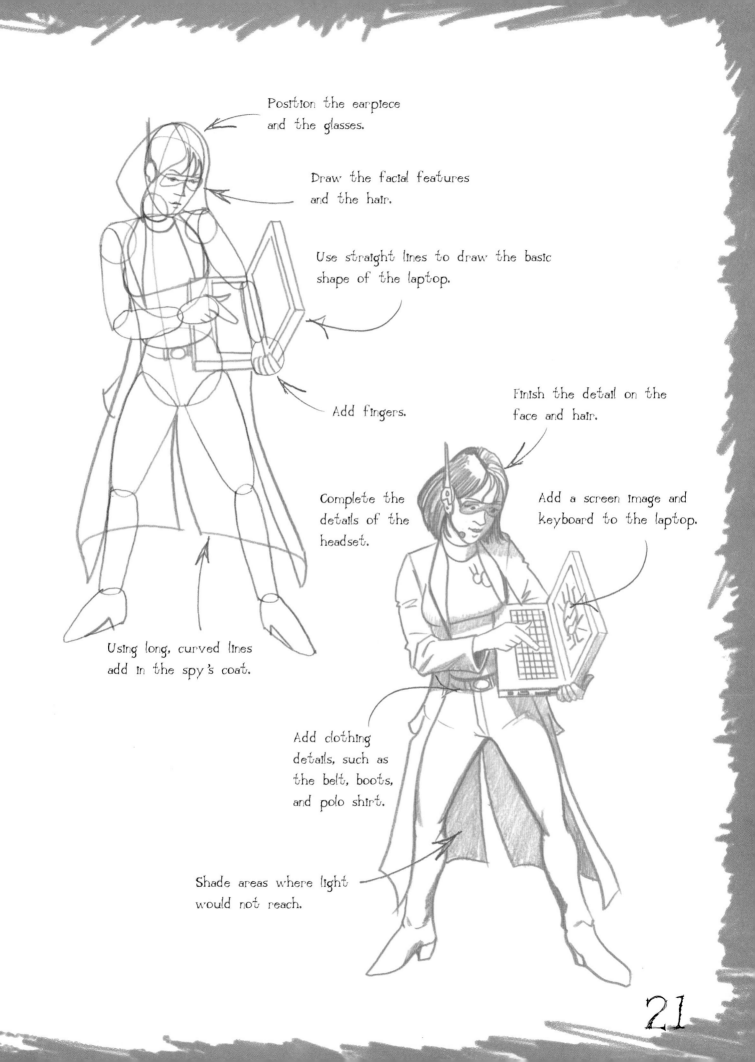

Position the earpiece and the glasses.

Draw the facial features and the hair.

Use straight lines to draw the basic shape of the laptop.

Add fingers.

Finish the detail on the face and hair.

Complete the details of the headset.

Add a screen image and keyboard to the laptop.

Using long, curved lines add in the spy's coat.

Add clothing details, such as the belt, boots, and polo shirt.

Shade areas where light would not reach.

Mutant Figure

T he mutant figure can be anything you can imagine. The figure here is a wolf man crouching on all fours and ready to attack!

Draw circles for the hips, body, neck, and head.

Hips

Neck

Head

Body

Draw two circles for the shoulders and connect them underneath with a straight line.

Sketch overlapping ellipses to create the legs.

Sketch the position of the feet.

Each arm is formed with two ellipses, a smaller one overlapping a larger one where they join.

Draw a large circle for each hand.

Mutant Heads

These mutant heads will give you some ideas for creating your own mutants!

22

Sketch small, jagged lines around the outlines of the wolf—man to indicate fur.

Draw two curved lines for the tail.

Sketch the basic facial features.

Add claw shapes to the back feet.

Draw the wolf man's sharp, pointed claws.

Complete the feet details.

Add V—shaped ears to the head.

Draw small overlapping lines to create the look of fur.

Draw the wolf man's leather harness.

Finish all the facial details.

23

Sci-Fi Warrior

The sci-fi warrior is a futuristic soldier with technologically-advanced armor and weaponry for fighting in the furthest reaches of the galaxy.

Start by drawing four ellipses: one each for the head, neck, torso, and hips. Add a curved center line.

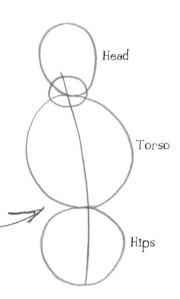

Head

Torso

Hips

Add two small circles on either side of the torso.

Add an oval to each arm for the hands.

Draw a line to position the laser gun.

Sketch the position of the arms with simple shapes that overlap at the joints.

Add curved lines for the top part of each leg.

Add straight lines for the lower part of each leg.

Draw the shape and direction of the feet.

24

Use construction lines as a guide to draw the basic shape and details of the helmet.

Draw the shape of the laser gun using straight lines.

Roughly sketch the shape of the fingers.

Add the jet pack on his back.

Add the body armor. Draw lines to indicate the joints in it.

Complete the details of the face and helmet.

Details like this circuit board can give the drawing a more futuristic look.

Draw sharp, spiky lines coming out of the end of the gun to create a dramatic effect.

Shade in areas where light would not reach.

Complete the details of the armor. All the shapes should be very precise.

25

Jungle Explorer

An expedition into the jungle can be very hazardous, so the explorer has to be ready for action. In this drawing, the explorer is swinging from a rope.

Head

Torso

Hips

Draw two circles connected by a line for the shoulders.

Draw a center line for the spine and add three circles for the head, torso, and hips.

Add rounded shapes for the arms that overlap at the shoulder and elbow joints.

Sketch larger, rounded shapes for the thighs.

Draw the lower legs with a simple tube shape, overlapping the top part of the leg to position the knee joints.

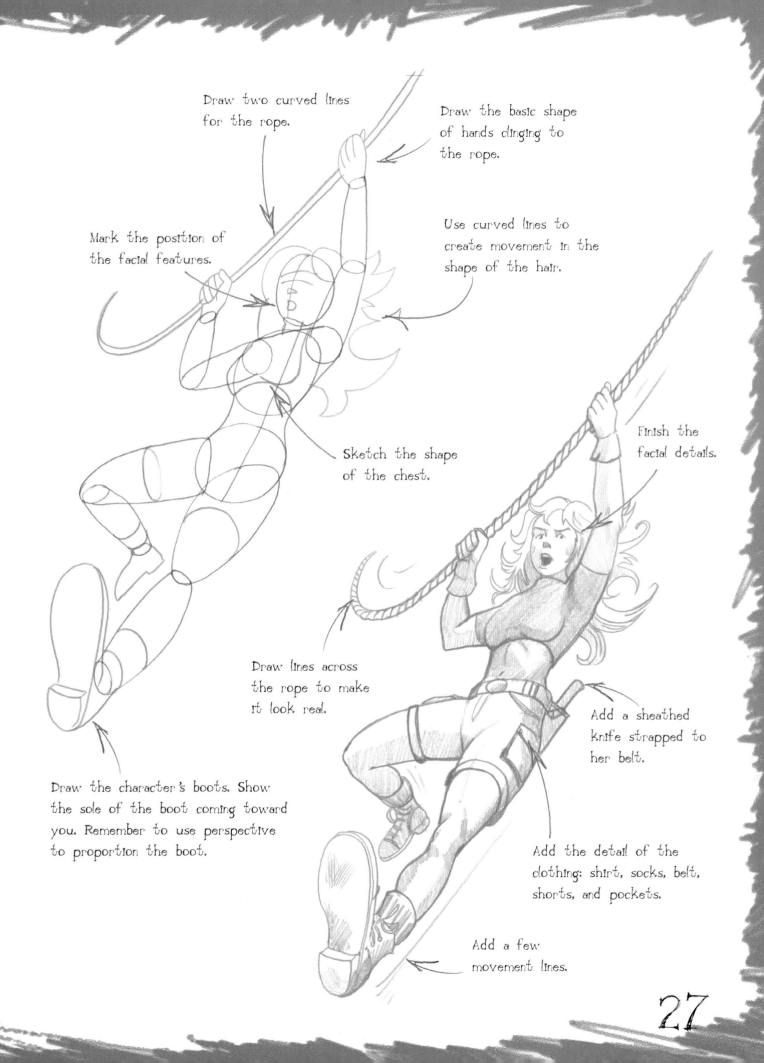

Draw two curved lines for the rope.

Draw the basic shape of hands clinging to the rope.

Mark the position of the facial features.

Use curved lines to create movement in the shape of the hair.

Sketch the shape of the chest.

Finish the facial details.

Draw lines across the rope to make it look real.

Add a sheathed knife strapped to her belt.

Draw the character's boots. Show the sole of the boot coming toward you. Remember to use perspective to proportion the boot.

Add the detail of the clothing: shirt, socks, belt, shorts, and pockets.

Add a few movement lines.

Cyborg

A cyborg is a combination of man and machine! With its mechanical additions, the cyborg is far faster and stronger than a human being.

Head

Torso

Hips

Draw simple shapes for the head, torso, and hips with a curved line for the spine. Add a line for the direction of the shoulders.

Draw an oval for the hand.

Sketch construction lines to give shape and direction to the head.

Extend the direction of the shoulder line forward. Now draw a long tube using perspective for the outstretched cybernetic arm.

Draw rounded, overlapping shapes for the legs.

Add the shape and direction of each foot.

Add detail to the normal arm.

Sketch the cybernetic eye and other facial features.

Add the jet pack, with flames shooting out from the bottom nozzles.

Draw mechanical features on the cybernetic arm.

Add a glove to this hand.

Finish the facial features.

Draw a laser beam coming from the cybernetic arm.

Add pants with pockets.

Complete the detail on the cybernetic arm. Try to make it as futuristic as possible!

Draw the boots.

Add shading to areas where light would not reach.

Martial Arts Warrior

The martial arts warrior defeats his foes using only his strength and his martial arts fighting technique. In this dramatic and action-filled pose, he is performing a flying kick.

Head

Torso

Hips

Draw rounded shapes for the head, neck, torso, and hips. Add a line for the spine.

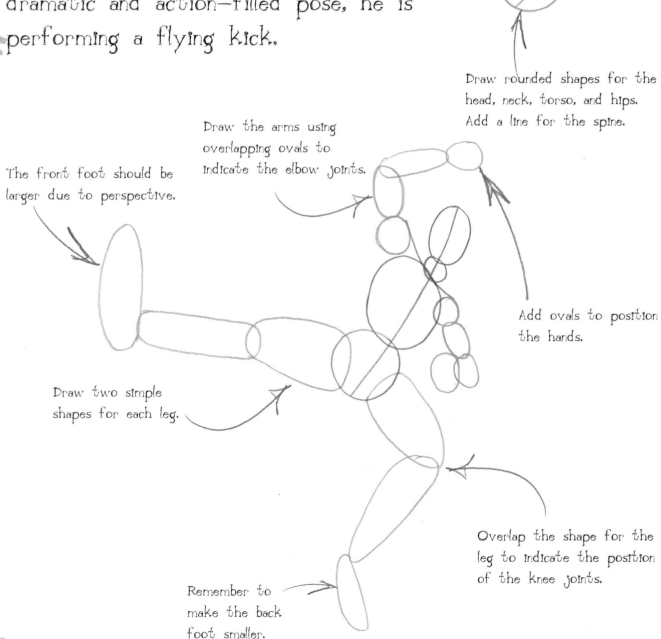

Draw the arms using overlapping ovals to indicate the elbow joints.

The front foot should be larger due to perspective.

Add ovals to position the hands.

Draw two simple shapes for each leg.

Overlap the shape for the leg to indicate the position of the knee joints.

Remember to make the back foot smaller.

Start to draw the muscle structure.

Make the position of the facial features and hair.

Using the construction lines as a guide draw both arms and fists.

Draw loose pants around the legs.

Draw the shape of the shoes.

Complete the details of the facial features and the hair.

Add tone to define the muscles.

Add muscles to both arms.

Add lines to indicate the movement of a flying kick.

Draw folds and creases on the pants.

Add shade to areas where light would not reach.

Glossary

center line (SEN-tur LYN) Often used as the starting point of the drawing, it marks the middle of the object or figure.

construction lines (kun-STRUK-shun LYNZ) Guidelines used in the early stages of a drawing and usually erased later.

fixative (FIK-suh-tiv) A type of resin used to spray over a finished drawing to prevent smudging. **It should be used only by an adult.**

perspective (per-SPEK-tiv) A method of drawing in which near objects are shown larger than faraway objects to give an impression of depth.

pose (POHZ) The position assumed by a figure.

proportion (pruh-POR-shun) The correct relationship of scale between each part of the drawing.

silhouette (sih-luh-WET) A drawing that shows only a flat dark shape, like a shadow.

sketchbook (SKECH-buhk) A book for making quick drawings.

vanishing point (VA-nish-ing POYNT) The place in a perspective drawing where parallel lines appear to meet.

Index

Web Sites